MIKE HARDING was born in Crump: into a working-class Irish-Catholic

His father was killed returning four weeks before Mike was born. on his childhood and later life and provided ... his haunting song 'Bombers' Moon'. Much of the inspiration for his writing comes from his early years growing up in Manchester.

After a chequered early career as a dustman, a bus conductor, a road digger and a carpet-fitter, Mike took a degree in Education, paying his way by singing and playing the guitar at night in folk clubs. Education took a back seat as he found his feet on the touring boards of the theatres and, instead of becoming a teacher as he had intended, he has had a half century of concert tours in these islands, as well as touring Australia, Hong Kong and the Middle East. Over the same period, he recorded more than 20 albums which still notch up impressive sales.

He has recorded 36 shows for BBC television attracting audiences of 4 to 8 million. Also with the BBC, he made a number of travel/eco programmes, including the series *The Harding Trail* where he cycled from Georgia to Louisiana filming old timey and jazz musicians along the way. He presented Folk, Roots and Acoustic Music on BBC Radio 2 from 1998 and 2012 and now presents a weekly folk show on the internet at www.mikehardingfolkshow.com.

In tandem with his public broadcasting life, Mike Harding has built a steady reputation as a writer and has earned widespread acclaim for both the quality and breadth of his work with close to 50 books published and plays performed. The bedrock running through all his work has been his poetry, his most recent collections of which include *Strange Lights Over Bexleyheath*, *The Connemara Cantos* and *Fishing for Ghosts* (all published by Luath Press). This latest collection, *Cosmos Mariner*, was described by one critic as 'his best work yet'.

He lives in both the north of England and a small cottage in Connemara.

Cosmos Mariner

MIKE HARDING

For Mathew
Best Wishes
Mike Harding
Settle
Jan 2020

Luath Press Limited

EDINBURGH

www.luath.co.uk

First published 2019

ISBN: 978-1-913025-34-2

The author's right to be identified as author of this book under the
Copyright, Designs and Patents Act 1988 has been asserted.

The paper used in this book is recyclable. It is made from low chlorine pulps
produced in a low energy, low emission manner from renewable forests.

Typeset in 11 point Sabon by Lapiz

Printed and bound by Bell & Bain Ltd., Glasgow

© Mike Harding 2019

MIX
Paper from
responsible sources
FSC® C007785
FSC
www.fsc.org

Contents

The Trainspotters

On the far ends of long platforms they watch the trains go by,
In mizzly, sad November, soft, heavy-eyed July;
Solemn, often bespectacled and almost always male,
Notebooks and pens in hand they scry the endless rails.

The weeping, sooty walls of some old halt or station
The backdrop to their duffle-bags and caps;
The sonorous words of Betjeman, Auden perhaps
Their lives' soundtrack. They have a bacon

Butty and a mug of builder's tea in the steamy buffet,
Then they're out again to stand all day like fixtures,
Their notebooks filled with times and engine numbers,
Their cameras crammed with pictures.

Pixels by the trillions of diesel trains,
Cross-countries, inter-cities, shunters;
For they are the most resolute of hunters –
Some engines, still it seems, are blessed with names.

I imagine them going home as evening washes in
To mothers who lovingly will knit them
Warm pullovers and socks with double heels,
Who cook them filling meat and two veg meals;
Who iron crisp, fresh sheets, who air their beds,
And check they have their waterproofs for the rain.

Yet, who am I to joke, sad poet on the train?
Filling my little book with words and lines instead
Of numbers; hoping for a namer or the odd, long freight
I know will have brought limestone from the hills?
I too am a collector who stays up far too late
Staring down the hopeful rails on dark nights, waiting still
For the word train to arrive – perhaps even the bonus of a steamer?
Poets and trainspotters, both – ever-hopeful dreamers.

MIKE HARDING

Nativity Play, Nice, France, Christmas 2018

A two-hundred-and-fifty-million-dollar yacht
Rides on a tide of money in the bay.
A fibreglass metropolis of greed and lights;
Ribbon reflections lick the water, snake and play
Across the gentle swell. We walk the promenade
And hear, coming from the ship, the music of a band;
A light soprano voice sings carols, soft and bright,
Descant of irony on this chill Christmas night.
There is a cutting edge to the onshore breeze,
Tonight the town sets in to freeze –
Trams jangle, hurrying homeward feet
Go blindly through the lit and emptying streets.

Under the unseeing eyes of mannequins
In fine coats and expensive dresses –
Comes a man, an infant, two years old I guess
With copper curls; the wife, a baby at her breast.

Not tramps or vagabonds, to me they look
Like ordinary people whose supply of luck
Has just run out. Painstakingly the man
Assembles bags, a buggy, blankets,
Turns a closed shop vestibule into a room;
And, on this ice-bright Christmas Eve,
As the indifferent, frost-spangled moon,
Haloed in this winter weather like a saint,
Rides high above the Christian sea and town,
They huddle close together and bed down.

No star-led Magi hurry here with gifts,
No ox, no ass, no choirs of angels sing,
No shepherds worship at this shop-door crib,
No room for the family here at any inn.

Cosmos Mariner – Destination Unknown

For Tony Curtis

What is a poet? Listen and I'll tell you. Long ago
I walked an old Savannah cemetery to a bluff where
    Spanish moss
Bearded a forest of cloud-bothering oaks, and far below
The great, old, muddy river dawdled. It was there I
    came across

A plain, stone, table tomb, on it the name, *Conrad Aiken*,
And the message, *Cosmos Mariner – Destination Unknown*.
The poet loved this place and lifted off from here, his soul
    now flown
Out somewhere far beyond the Painter's Easel constellation.

Who knows? Perhaps old Conrad made it to the very end,
To the wall where all the flux of time and matter dies.
Cosmos Mariner? It was a ship. The poet knew his boats,
    would spend
The sun-downs sat here with his wife, Mary, a thermos flask
    of iced

Mint julep and some crackers in a grip. He loved the laggard
    river's motion,
The heave and fret of freighters threading shoals for distant
    oceans.
He'd raise his glass in blessing to the mariners on deck
Then carefully note down each vessel's name. Back home he'd
    check

The shipping news to find which seaports they were
    making for:
London, Sydney, Bombay, Valparaíso, Singapore.
But for the Cosmos Mariner there was no landfall shown,
No final shore, no safe haven, just 'destination unknown'.

So Conrad carved his epitaph from these things:
    a passing boat,
And a snip of shipping news – two small gobbets
    of rhymer's gold.
By alchemy, they melded and the amalgam made
A fine conundrum for the passer-by, a puzzle for
    a poet's grave.

So that's what poets are: word-peckers, rhyming jackdaws
    of the world,
Beachcombers turning flotsam (with a sailor's luck) to pearls.

The Million Dollar Fiddle

*The sounds of people drowning are something that I cannot
describe to you, and neither can anyone else. It's the most dread-
ful sound and there is a terrible silence that follows it.*
EVA HART, Second Class Survivor, ss Titanic (Lifeboat 14)

No priceless Stradivarius with its secret, sunset bloom,
But a German factory fiddle in a White Star concert room.
A gift from his fiancé – *Bon voyage Wally! All the best!*
But when they later found it, strapped across the tacet chest
Of fiddler Wallace Hartley, fished from the icy waves
From amongst the flotsam, fur coats, deckchairs, tables,
Children's toys and empty lifeboats, that fiddle played
Its way, in time, into another fable.

They say that when they knew all hope was gone
The dance band on the Titanic just played on,
Notes flying out into the icy, sparkling night
To calm the passengers. It was light and tight,
Of course, strict tempo, steady as the screech
Of Morse. Jack Phillips from Godalming
Was drumming out relentless in the wireless room,
Ditt ditt ditt, dah dah dah, ditt ditt ditt,
Ditt ditt ditt, dah dah dah, ditt ditt ditt,
In 9/8 time, a neat enough slip jig.

We all now, in our mind's eye, see those little stars
Of bulbs snuffed on that murderous arctic night,
As the triumphal, celestial, city of light,
Certain sure and double-bound for glory,
Up-ends and slides beneath the waves.
And, then and there, the tales of all the people come
Together, prince and pauper, in one last story.

The democratic cusp of iceberg and steel hull,
Observed no niceties of class or wealth.
Providence, jigging to the music of the band and gulls,
Hovered like a paraclete with freezing breath,
And gathered gold-toothed playboy, gambling man,
Housemaid, banker, heiress, ragtime band
And peat bog 'Paddy' by the hand,
And danced them to a frozen, terrible death.

'Even God can't sink her', it was claimed.
Well sink she did and that was just the overture
To the great unravelling of all our sureties.
Old Europe soon was digging its own grave,
Sinking Kaisers, states and empires in
A tide of trenches reaching from the Channel to the Alps.
Another arrogant, well designed, Titan machine
Would founder in a sea of truth and mud,
And sink so many million lives and dreams.

And now someone, a century later, pays
A million dollars for that salty violin;
Because perhaps, like a death's head on a tomb,
That fiddle, on that April night became
A symbol of the death of something more:
The smug Darwinian creed made manifest that Man
Had come, through his great works, to be the Lord of all.

That dead man floating with the fiddle
On his chest, and that ghost ship, torment us still,
Hang over us like a pall;
And now, like children with the bogeyman,
We are left with constant nightmares
Of a burning planet and the Fall.

The Cleggan Sonettinas

I The Cuckoo at Cloon

Before I forget let me remember them,
Those mornings when the bright May sun
Was high over the Bens coaxing the dew
From off the haggard. I would stand
At the half-door, laggard like,
A mug of strong tea in my hand,
To smell the sea, turf smoke, the new grass.
There I would listen to the urgent wood-flute song:
Like an ocarina blown breath-soft.
Two notes; you in the woodland
Calling, looking for a mate,
Me at the half-door looking out with hope
For the coming of summer,
The coming of hope.

II Rose Hips, Fountain Hill

Each summer we would return, fresh off the boat,
Drive out beyond Omey, St Féchín's Isle,
That twice a day is islanded by the tide.
We would take the narrow lane just at the pole
With the ESB box, where the red tractor
Was always in the yard.
Then we would park, and walk the *bóirín*
To the sea. Harebells in the grass and, all along,
The blown-glass, blood beads of the hips.
All through your growing years,
Always the rose hips and always the waves.

And once a dog chased in and out the sea,
Barked at the rollers, bit at the foam I told you
Was the little fishes' ice cream, and you believed.

III Máirtín and the Loaves and Fishes

A glorious day in summer, then over the hill
Came visitors, good friends and family – their orbits kissed
And numbers went beyond the empty fridge.
We opened wine, small children ran around,
I wondered about the meal to come:
The pub? A quick trip into town?
Over the hill – a vision, Saint Máirtín with
A well-filled fertiliser bag. Before I had a chance
Even to say 'Hello', the words came in a shout,
'Now! Would ye like a feed of mackerel?'
We got out the paper dishes, lit the charcoal,
And raised a glass to salad, bread and fishes,
Wine and sun and friendship,
And the Blessed Máirtín and his miracle gift.

IV Big Bill

Big hands you daily used for getting tunes
From valves and U-bends, pumps and pipes;
All day you played at plumbing,
But then, by God, at night,
The wire and wood transmuted by
Those self-same fingers sent such notes into the air.
I see you sitting by the turf fire still
In Newman's vamping the jazz chords;
Like Peerie Willie Johnson, Big Bill could walk
The walk. Oh, what nights we had, man!
Doing it because we could and feck

The begrudgers! Big man with laughing eyes
You left a hole in time and space,
A *tacet*, larger Bill, than you will ever know.

v Christy & the Half-Door

We left the half-door open and played tunes,
Friends of so many years. The breakfast done,
The dishes in the sink, and more tea made.
Guitar and mandolin, we sat and sang and played
That summer morning. As though called by the tunes
A neighbour wandered in and sat to listen,
Natural as a bee settling on a flower:
This cottage was always a music house.
And it was easy as loving that bright hour.
Hot strong tea, the half door, friendship,
Tunes and the craic and, 'Feck it!'
It made me want to shout,
'When you weigh it all up really,
What all else is life about?'

vi Like Rocks the People

Solid. Quartz menhirs stud the bog,
Stone lines point to where the full moon lips
The Bens; dolmens, ritual rocks. Solid.
Like the hands of Jimmy Mullen,
His long fingers hardly moved
Gripping the fiddle's neck,
Yet pouring the sweet music out
Like porter from a jug –
Music that could make a dead man dance.
Solid as gentle Frank King and his saxophone
Lashing out the jigs and reels

And finishing with 'Stranger on the Shore'.
'All music's music,' he once said. Aye Frank,
In the after hours, on the broad strand
Of the welcoming mind.

VII   John G

You know the way some things can feel just right?
The way the sun dips over Bofin
On a summer's night; the laugh of a small child,
Or a blackbird hitting those sweet, eternal,
Flawless notes that would bring tears from a stone?
So it was with John G and his tunes:
The fingers on the buttons sending music
Round the room, nothing ever wasted,
Not a boastful phrase or showy roll;
Just rooted, slotted in his music
Like the sun laying down the beach,
Living in the notes, never going
Out beyond his reach. Just like John G himself.
A gentle man, fierce music. Steady, deep.

The Killing Field Scheherazade

In a field whose crop was innocent souls condemned to die,
Each morning, the young boy with the slaughterhouse eyes
Would choose the ones whose lives would end that day.
Chained like a rosary they'd then be dragged away,
To change that morning world for endless night,
Under a silent sun, a mute, indifferent sky.

There was one man he always spared,
As long as he'd a story still to sell. Each dawn
The teenage angel of death would come from Hell
To listen, as the storyteller spun out Aesop's words
To tell the beads of a word-won day of life:
Fables of grapes and storks, the cunning fox,
Of the boy who shouted wolf, of the crow, the ox;
Of hares and tortoises, of lions, mice, crabs, owls
Of grasshoppers and crabs, and frogs who wished
    for a King.

A killing field Scheherazade, he stretched
Old Aesop's stories artfully out, gilding
Each day's tale with nuance, shade and character,
Making the fox more shifty and the crow
More vain; even the hare was given its own name.
And so he cast them out and reeled them in, playing
His executioner like a shark, day after fearful day,
Paying for each new morning with another tale.

Somehow the raft of fables kept the man afloat
All through those lunatic days, with luck he sailed
Across that mocking sea of skulls, until his boat

Of words made landfall and, war's end, there was no more.
Then wearing his own dark, new, wondrous tale
Like a storyteller's many-coloured cloak, he stepped ashore.

This true story came from Andrew Cayley, international co-prosecutor for the UN at the Khmer Rouge Tribunal between 2009 and 2013. The storyteller survived to become his translator.

From a Railway Carriage

I look out of the window as we trundle down the rails;
Land slides to winter, logs are stacked
Against the backs of houses, and slow waves
Of fog fail in the morning's strengthening sun. Jack
Frost feathers hedges, blanches meadows, furs
The wires that swoop and rise beside the track.
Our slow train trundles on, the land outback
Smudged, mist-marbled, pale. Far flatlands shelf
To the edge of seen, a stalking line of pylons,
A troop of arrogant iron men marches to the lost horizon.
A Norman tower stands high above some -ton
Or -by or -ham. Then it too is gone.

And England rolls on by: red wreaths before
A cenotaph, people still clinging for a while
To the hope, somehow, that all the killing
Had a point beyond the mercantile;
Was more than just a Turk's Head knot of lies,
The figures on a leather-bound ledger's page
In some city's cotton, coal or corn exchange.

Impossible, slender spires needle their way
To heaven, standing in their stone silos
Over river plains and gentle swelling wolds;
Wool made them, wool and monks, back in the day.
They prospered before both tides and favour turned;
Then choirs were silenced and great abbeys burned.
And now, this very English scene is set perhaps to die,
The power and glory melting like the morning mist,
The empty churches raise their stone fists to a hollow sky.

Ribs of ploughed fields, small huddled farms,
Dead tractors, four-by-fours, outhouses, barns

With rusting roofs, allotments – the great hurl,
And lob and heft and clutter of the world.
We trundle past whole lives;
In that house is someone dying,
A field away someone is being born.

Then, as we slow to a crawl, there comes
The coming of the hills, the woods, the old ways in;
The aspens, silver birch, the edges of the wild,
Uncivil, gnawbone, brambled, thorn-toothed raw.
And on the very edge of the edge, at the open door
Of a solitary wheel-less caravan on bricks,
Woodsmoke curling from its pipe, well off the grid,
A man sits, smoking, watching, by his side, a lurcher dog,
In front of him a woodpile and an axe stuck in a log.

And for a sliver of time our eyes and minds
Meet in some understanding; something passes
Through the freezing air and glass; in that quiet place,
That moment we are fixed together in that flash,
That brief juncture of time and space.
And it is this: that man, that dog, that day
I know I will remember now always;
As, like two dancers on an empty ballroom floor,
We pick up pace along our shining lines
And waltz apart to the hurrying music of time.

The Last Tramp in all England

I'm happy in the summertime beneath the bright blue sky,
Nae thinkin' in the mornin' at nicht whaur I've tae lie
TRAMPS AND HAWKERS – a folk song

What told me that day was the gait,
A gimp right out of time, halfway
Between a shamble and a march,
Along the lonely road that crossed the parched
High summer moors. He humped a bag, head bare,
A hermit's beard, clagged ginger hair,
Old army boots, grass and newspaper socks,
An army coat; walk-dreaming of a hay-barn bed,
A brew drummed up, thick slice of bread,
A rabbit skinned and ready for the pot.

He tramped the road over a Pennine pass,
In a bowl of blooming heather, broom and sky
Under a canopy of lark song, a lone rover.
I remember now how I drove
At a crawl to get a better look at him – the last
Tramp in all England. Alone, shunning
The towns, keeping to fields and moors;
Slipping through the fingers of suburbia –
Odd jobs for a few bob and a cup of tea.
Threading the avenues and cul-de-sacs,
Small gardens, with crabbed bungalows,
Herbaceous borders, garden gnomes;
Little England, snug and smug, sleeping
On this hot, dry day, keeping
To the creed that all is well; Duty,
Queen and Country.
            And through it

All would march a serious question mark:
The last tramp in all England, Jimmy No-job.
No-clock, ambling on his way, seeing no one,
Happy enough with silence and
Content to simply be, to ramble 'till he died.
The road his home, a dry ditch for a bed;
He sleeps roofed by the stars, hugged by
The rattle-bone arms of a hawthorn hedge.

And still he walks through England
In the mirror of my mind,
Tramping alone the starlit miles,
The last tramp of his kind.
A pilgrim, seeking no shrine
But the ever-open road;
Rambling on, only content
When his face was turned
To the hills and the sky
And away from the world of men.

King Cotton

The proletarian is, therefore, in law and in fact, the slave of the bourgeoisie, which can decree his life or death. It offers him the means of living, but only for an 'equivalent' for his work.
FRIEDRICH ENGELS – *The Condition of the Working Class in England*

1 The Song of the Cobbles

They paved the Savannah waterfront
With cobbles lifted from the Salford streets,
Ballast for the cotton boats returning home
Slack-bellied from the hungry looms of Lancashire.
So now the cracked, black soles of slavery's feet
Will dance upon the best dressed Pennine stone.

On a Sunday those same feet will cakewalk, strut
Their stuff in red clay dust to the yawl of fiddle,
The plack of banjos and the hoom of jugs.
While, over the waves, King Cotton's subjects come
To Cottonopolis to live in Bondage Street.
They come in thousands in submission,
From the land, the moors, the bog – all driven
By their bellies. Down in floods they wash, swilled
From towns and villages, from dales and hills.

Hard as any master's lash cold famine cracks its whip
And drives the beggared Irish to the emigrant ship.
They line the docks at Dublin waiting for a berth,
A coat of *Béarla beag* upon their tongues.
The poorest travel free as ballast on coal boats
And die in storms coffined in battened down holds.
Those that live walk barefoot, two long days

Towards the smoke and scrow of Manchester,
To live in new built slums where the mortar is still wet,
To live in Angel Meadow with the cockroaches and rats.

A brass band plays so sweet somewhere
As cotton lint dances in the Salford air,
And falls like warm snow on
The black curls of the jug band's hair.

Brick forests of tall chimneys spool out smoke
As though to weave the clouds; the Pennine hills
Flash water from the moors down to the mills;
Redbrick ships, they sail above a sea of smoky streets.
Like ships the mills have names: *Hope, Victory, Albion,*
Prosperous, Egypt, India, Paragon.
Black rivers sing the song of money being spun
And a choir of factory hooters yowl and bray
To call the citizens of nowhere out into the day.

Men and women, undersized and sick
Slip factory-bound through unlit streets;
Children hurry to the mill their clogs clatter
Teeth chatter in the pale chill dawn.
Small hands, bare feet, hurry between the looms
Service the iron beasts in the weaving rooms.
Hunger gnawing, sleep-starved, yawning, never dare
    to slack,
And always there: the overlooker at your back.

And in the red clay, bending, harvesting the bolls,
The small, black feet cakewalk the red clay rows,
And little hands reach up in waves to pick
The cotton buds, and cram their sacks;
And always there: the overseer's whip
Ready to lick your well-striped back.

A brass band plays so sweet somewhere
As cotton floss flecks the Salford air,
And falls like clock o' clay upon
The black curls of the jug band's hair.

II Let Us Consider the Lives of Famous Men

Here Marx and Engels, in frockcoats,
Promenade the quiet Sunday streets
From Pomona Gardens to the Bailey Bridge,
Each with a young girl on his arm; Irish,
Sisters, Mary and Lizzie Burns,
Just one step from the Famine ditch.
Minds sharp as needles they sew the fine stitch
Of anarchy, talk of the hungry poor, the hell
They work and live in; of capital, revolt,
And liberty from the bullying factory bell.
They pass the great new temples to King Cotton,
The counting houses, offices, the Doric columns
Of the Cotton Exchange, the city eating
Its way outwards, its vast stone and iron mouth
Eats all it will, and shits at will, just where it will.

A jug band plays a ragtime tune,
And dancers cakewalk in the Georgia moon,
As lint falls like snow upon
The wage slaves in the great mill rooms.

A short walk from the Cotton Exchange is Irish Town;
The girls lead Engels through the slums and down
Through midden pools of piss and shit, dead dogs
And cats, and further down to cellars where
The children of the dead end and the hogs
Sleep side by side. They go to drinking dens and whorehouses

In Angel Meadow where the angels are all black
With smoke and slutch. They go through tenements
Where babies, high on laudanum, stare
With still, unblinking and unseeing eyes
At skies dulled with the smoke from Arkwright's Mill.
In this most savage slum, the children play
At football with the human skulls they find
In the old burial ground and scavengers glean
Dog shit for the Tanyard pits, bones for
The glue works. Here thirty thousand swarm
In the reeking labyrinth of Old King Cotton's pleasure dome;
And Engels writes his notes while holding a cologne
Soaked handkerchief pressed to his nose.
Eyes wet with nausea and pity, he holds his breath
To dim the stench of hunger, money and death.

Marx and Engels meet in Chetham's house of books
To write and smoke and talk of revolution.
Close by the Irwell slides, slinks, stinks, polluted,
Chameleon-like, coloured by up-river aniline dyes.
It is silvered with dead salmon; they float by
In great rafts; coal tar crusts their gills, bloated
And festering. They swam two thousand miles
From Greenland, come back to spawn,
Seeking the high, clear streams where they were born.
They, like the Irish, swam into a stream of misery
And poison in a river that boiled with scurf and foam,
And now they roll and rot downriver to the sea.

At their small table in the library, Marx makes
His notes and listens as Engels talks about his book;
From that small room the echoes sound
That given time will turn the world around.

A jug band plays a ragtime tune,
And dancers cakewalk in the Georgia moon,
As lint falls like soft snow upon
The wage slaves in the great mill rooms.

III   In the Throne Room of the Cotton King

King Cotton sits enthroned in stone and brass
In a city made from steam and cotton bolls,
Smoke and coal and pride and greed and glass,
Streets cobbled with the tears of broken souls.
Its pillars the weavers' wish-bone legs,
Its walls the spinners' children's cries,
Its windows the miners' jagged breath,
Its roof the foul, smoke-devilled sky.

And down in Old Savannah are rich squares
Of Antebellum mansions, Palladian, Italianate
And Regency with tree-cool boulevards. Everywhere
Old Europe has laid its thumbprint on the New
World, and, as in Angel Meadow,
There is bondage for the many –
The wine of life, and liberty to drink it for the few.

Flanders lace, parasols, silks, bustles, ribboned hair;
Wrought iron curlicues, white Apuan marble stairs;
Pediments, Ionic columns, and within:
Dresden china, Murano glass, pianos from Berlin,
Best Belfast linen, Turkish rugs and ottomans,
Mahogany armoires, gilded furniture from France.

Under the Southern sun old Colonel Money walks,
And in the elegant squares he stops to talk,
Raising his hat and taking silk-gloved hands,
As the new made Titans walk their promised land,
With bows and curtsies, a nod to the jaunting cars,
With 'How do you do's, 'Good morning's,
And the sweet-smelling cigars.
And Colonel Money sleeps at night in marble vaults
Where he fears only the weevil and the slave revolt.

The bolls of Georgia floss picked by black slaves
Are trading figures in Manchester's Cotton Exchange –
'The biggest room in all the world' –
Before they've left the old Savannah docks.
Landed in Liverpool, the bales are barged
Along the Duke's Cut to the vats and cogs
Of Cottonopolis. Cotton, steam and smoke,
That's what King Cotton eats, and he drinks the sweat
And blood of half a million souls.
Soft water from the hills, moist air to ease the threads;
Deep underneath the land a million tonnes
Of coal waiting, above, a million spindles waiting,
A million shuttles waiting, ready for the King to come.

Valves hiss, shuttles clatter, looms yammer,
The wage slaves lip-read in the dumbing clamour.
The bent-legged tribe, a people doomed
To fill the hive and drudge their lives
Under the same stars as the rich,
Rise to the factory siren, the plantation bell.

Each dawn in Hell: the natter and cackle of clogs,
The spirit-sucking and soul-eating toil;
The bare feet on the red-clay soil.
At night the slaves search the sky to where
The Plough, the Drinking Gourd, points to the north
And freedom, could they run. But there are chains
On the black legs, and chapel chains on souls.

IV The Big Ship Sails Through the Alley Alley Oh

They dig a ditch to bring the ships the forty miles
Into the city's belly on a sliver of sea;
Big men of Manchester, the Cotton Lords

The Dukes and Barons of the old fat King,
Come down in their fine carriages to see
The navvies shovel muck, eat dirt, shit brass,
Wheel clay, piss gold, drink down the lime.
And the Empress of India travels one last time
To her northern realm to cut the tape,
And celebrate her empire's newest wonder
And thank God for his bounty – and so it comes to pass.

And the children of the New Jerusalem come
To watch the Yankee ships being shepherded by tugs.
They walk the great new docks to see the big
Ships looming over terraced red-brick streets.
That spread in rows across the ghosts of fields.

And the children dance
Under the bunting and the flags,
And sing,

The big ship sails through the alley alley oh
The alley alley oh
The alley alley oh
The big ship sails through the alley alley oh
On the first day of September.

'The Ships are Sailing into Salford'
The artistes belt it out each night upon the limelit stage
At the Empire, Theatre Royal, the Regent and the Vic;
In theatre, pub and music hall the song is all the rage;
While in the cabins on the swamp's dark edge,
As June bugs spark and burning crosses bark and bless
The Southern dirt, they sing of Diamond Joe
And halts and stations on the underground railroad.

A brass band plays, Begone Dull Care,
As cotton lint flits through the Salford air,
And flecks like strange white moths
The black curls of the jug band's hair.

Savannah's floss transmuted, steam ships
Sail from Salford streets down the Big Cut
And out across the Mersey Bar.
The spider king spools on, sending his web –
Damask, gingham, percale, poplin, calico,
Velvet, dhootie, chambray – out across the world.
A million spindles turn, a million shuttles fly,
And still the cotton spider spews and curdles,
Spins a million miles a day, the moon and back four times.
Leviathan, he swallows people, eats their lives,
Their towns, whole fields and rivers – a behemoth –
A quarter of the world wears Old King Cotton's cloth.

And the Captains and the Lords,
The Colonels and their corn-fed wives,
The great men in their mansions in the hills,
The great men in the groves of Spanish moss,
Live high above the rat-damp alleys and the other lives,
The red brick, stinking, swarming hives,
Live far from the singing, clamorous swamps.

They bless their own good fortunes,
All justified by faith;
God smiles upon the prosperous,
The poor must know their place.
In whitewashed clapperboard churches,
Smoke-blackened Zion chapels,
They laud and sing hosannahs to their god.

And in the sheds the weavers kiss the shuttle,
The little doffers barefoot scuttle,
And the bobbins turn, the loom bars rattle,
The lam jacks, jinny gates dance and prattle;
The hands pick, pluck and weave and spin,
And the boats sail out and the boats sail in.

A jug band plays a ragtime tune,
And the dancers cakewalk in the Georgia moon,
As lint falls like snow upon
The wage slaves in the great mill rooms.

v   The King Is Dead

And yet now, fast as he came, King Cotton's gone
With Old King Coal, Prince Iron and the Chemical Queen,
Dead as Delaney's Donkey buried deep;
You would hardly know their kingdoms once
Were here. The mineshafts filled, pit heads
Grassed over; warehouses, weaving sheds,
The great mills – under the wrecking ball or turned to flats.
Old King Cotton – dodo-dead. Just like that.
The last day's trading figures still stand high
And frozen on the marble walls
Of the Old King's Palace, The Royal Exchange.
Angel Meadow – flattened by Hitler's bombs
And now, a tiny city park; the Ragged School still stands,
And outlet malls squat on the stone-built past.

Preening architects glide through meeting rooms,
In the Town Hall, their Powerpoint juju flashes on the screens
As a tawdry, manic Manc Oz climbs skywards,
Skinned anew in Old King Money's coat
Of greed and concrete, steel and glass.
'Manhattan on the Irwell' they now cry,
And, Cottonopolis long gone,
The glass cocks built with foreign brass climb on
Towards the smoke-untroubled sky.
And, beneath the money towers, the chrysalids
Of the homeless hunker for the winter's night
In sleeping bags on cardboard beds. Come light,
Come dawn some may well hatch, imagos

Shuffling off or begging with their dogs;
Some won't make it through; Deansgate
Cocoons, unmoving, no butterflies; stilled rags,
Untroubled by the clatter of work-bound feet.

Money making money; nothing really made
Here now; the forges, mills, the dyeworks,
Steel works, foundries, pits – all gone
As though it was a dream. And now it seems
At times a battlefield after a war,
With the wounded and the bodies everywhere,
But there are stories in the soil and stone, unburied;
The sense of something gone, hurried
Away, as though a great storm wind has come
And has flown screaming through the north
And scraped and scoured away a people's history.

And away in Old Savannah
Strong-hearted Hannah,
Now vamps the old Joanna.
Her slim, black fingers dancing on the keys
She tickles cakewalks, ragtime tunes
From the old Edwardian ivories;
And the coach tours come to listen
On the Salford-cobbled quays.
They eat their pretzels and ice creams,
And watch the great new cargo ships,
As the eternal, muddy river
Dawdles to the innocent sea.

Landfall, Small Island, Outer Hebrides

For George Monbiot; fighter, truth-teller.

Out of the heave and huck of the world we sailed,
As smooth as butter, coasting our slow way
Into a small, still cove, landfall in haven bay.
Sun, lingering in the last kiss of the day,
Flushed a flock of small, high clouds out west
Turning them to copper, cream and molten brass.

Inland amongst high trees there was a manse
Where a poet lived, a learned man who had
The Gaelic and who saved the *muckle sangs*
Glad-gifted from the islanders, offered up,
Their music loved and nurtured, cupped
Close in their sea-worn, singing hands
Like rare and fragile sea birds' eggs.

Inching our way inshore to drop anchor
We slid into a slick, a great lagoon, a canker
Of plastic bottles, polystyrene floats,
Fish crates, torn nets, blue nylon ropes,
And fertiliser bags, a great, thick film
That filled the bay; acres of the sick, slack money-scum
Spew of our Bedlam world sloughed here.

And there we moored and walked the strand,
As the day slipped towards the edge of light;
A ruined chapel on the far headland,

MIKE HARDING

The first stars pricking the dimming sky.
And we heard from off the hill a curlew calling
Its fluting song filling the softening dusk,
And all about, moving with the slack tide, falling
And rising – the thick crust of the leprosy of us.

Catastrophy

Life's going to be melted down all over the world.
EM FORSTER – *Howards End*

I held a council at 10.45 to declare war with Germany, it is a
terrible catastrophy (sic) *but it is not our fault.*
KING GEORGE V in his diary, August 1914

Five men made that war:
Haldane, Lloyd George,
Asquith, McKenna, Grey.
A few more helped perhaps,
A bunkered clique that day
Conjured it all up, pure stage magic;
They sawed a woman in three halves and slick
Produced two bunnies from each shining topper.

Proper job they did: drum bangers,
Mob risers, haranguers,
Death's guisers. Just five
Determined powerful men,
Shitting out the lies:
'The German threat!' and 'War is good,
Will cleanse us all!' 'The sacrifice of blood
Just like dear Christ's will wash away the old
Bring in the pure, bright new; as in a flood'.

A day later – the first war cabinet talked
Of dishing out the spoils, nobody baulked.
German East Africa, South West Africa,
Togoland, the Cameroons, as though it all
Was no more deadly than a country walk,
A choir outing or a jolly trip to France.

And still the pier-end Pierrots sang and danced
Their ragtime, banjo jigs, hopping
On the sawdust from the coffin-maker's shop.

We know now that, by Christ's Mass,
All of Europe was held fast, checkmated in the mud.
Soon there were no voices raised against the blood
That were not 'saboteurs!' or 'traitors!'
White feathers handed out and few that had the guts
To call the king-and-country madness. All it took:
The Old School Song, a King and lies and fear –
The greatest cocktail in the eternal barman's book.

Adlestrop Revisited

I remember the name because, short of the halt,
The slow train gave a sudden jolt – then stopped.
I wiped the window and looked out. Somebody coughed
And shook a newspaper. The snow stretched far
As I could see; a curve of woodland and a little farm
Were way off in the failing light, grey, soft and pearl
That smoothed the edges of our little world.

The dull, steel sky, not yet owning the evening,
Told us nothing, only it was winter
And was getting late. No birds sang, a solitary crow
Scratched across the sky, loping towards its roost.
There was no announcement,
No one came, no one went;
We were somewhere in the middle. Blocked.

Then something began, something was coming near.
People running, hobbled by the snow,
Hurrying from that distant, solitary farm.
First came a rag tag bunch, unarmed;
Women, children, men? It was hard to tell.
Some stumbled as they ran, snow-snared and fell.
Then came men more purposeful,
With guns, in uniforms I didn't recognise.
The hunters knelt, took aim and fired,
Shots rapped and barked, there were soul-dark cries
And the quarry, puppets with cut wires,
Stopped running and fell down;
On the snow, blood-flowers spread all around.
We saw now that the farmhouse was ablaze,
The land around it blushing with the glow,
And where they fell, the people just erased
Were sinking slowly down into the snow.

MIKE HARDING

It was then the men in uniforms
Studied our halted train.
Our breath misted the windows
We dared not wipe it off. Nobody came,
Nobody went, nobody cracked the air with words;
And all around us stretched the curve
Of woodland, burning farm and snow.
A darkening silence, no birds sang
Just that one, lone, circling carrion crow
Watching stories being written on the land.

That First Step

Just picture it: the rising sun
Kisses the good, sweet earth, and tips
Your bayonet. Your dry, cracked lips
Still burning from the double tot of rum
Hold a shaky woodbine, you look down the line –
Grey faces stare, unseeing, across the wire;
The whistle blows to start the fun,
You curse the liars and generals, not the Hun,
And clutch the pygmy's straw that is your gun.

But that first step – just how the fuck
Did they all do it? Off the duck
Boards, shaking legs, stumble up the steps,
To a bumbled, shit-scared scramble over the parapets.
And then the officers' 'Walk, don't run!'
They went mindlessly into the yammering,
Wailing wall of gas and shells and lead;
They ambled, those lost boys
Into the Kingdom of the Dead.

Lads from the shires and towns,
Lads from the factories and downs,
Lads from the Dales and the harbours,
Sons and brothers, husbands, fathers,
Lads from the townlands and the glens
That will never see the dawn again.

Half a million pals and mates,
Half a million souls in khaki, 'for a lark'
Went strolling into Hell's amusement park.
And the great machine then dealt with them
As neat and accurate as any lathe or loom
Or threshing machine – rattling out all the while
The metal howls of battle, industrial style.

MIKE HARDING

And all for what? For lies and money
As all the wars are for;
For lies and money
And the secret doctrines of the rich.

And the names in brass and stone
Will tell you nothing, only say
That one fair day they marched away,
And that they didn't come home.

And though there was for them great change
That day as they were turned to burned, ripped meat –
Blinded, made mad, gassed, crippled, shot and lamed;
Though telegrams would come down quiet country lanes
And busy, smoky, narrow, city streets –
The tills still rang, the birds sang sweet,
Somewhere a ploughman turned his team
With singing brass and heavy, clay-shod feet,
And didn't hear his brother's scream.

Still city men were dining at the Ritz,
And still the trading figures clicked
In all the great exchanges of the world,
That lovely morning as the murder and the day unfurled.

But that first step – just how the fuck
Did they and all their pals walk out into the shining day,
Knowing agony and endless night was just one chuck
Of the dice, one card, one kiss of Lady Luck away?

Fool's Gold

Deep in a great rainforest's secret core,
Along the silver strand of a silent lake,
They found a bone-white city, deserted on the shore,
Home now only to sloths, to poison frogs and snakes.

It has been conquered by the vegetable world,
Its blood-splashed idols have grown beards and capes,
And the patient fingers of the greening years have curled
And picked and split the fine, dressed stone. Now apes
Hold court in echoing rooms, patrolling panthers come
To stalk this silent city; built by a people with no name,
Who cut their children up and fed them to the sun.

Beneath the dead metropolis the searchers found a cave,
Where an army of forgotten, nameless hands,
Two thousand years ago and more, had made
A perfect microcosm of their world above;
A replica white city, with pyramids knee-high
Great towers and palaces, temples and squares. All lie
In faultless miniature, a model maker's dream, made
With every detail cut and carved and scribed;
With flowers of polished gems and trees of solid jade.

The stone sky, cavern roof, that spans this underworld,
Is studded with Fool's Gold, cut cubes of
Iron Pyrites set in the rock to mimic stars; they burn
And glitter in a perfect sky-map of the night above.

Pooled on the floor a Lilliput lake of mercury lies,
Mirrors the constellations in the cave's black sky;
In this waveless pool the Fool's Gold glistens,
While all about the torchlit silence listens.

And over this great city a mask of Death stares down:
A giant, obsidian skull with turquoise eyes, a crown
Of silver, fluorite, topaz and abalone
And teeth carved delicately out of human bone.

Yet all of this – this hymn to power and wealth,
This testament to the great ambitions of the wise,
The vision of astrologers and architects and priests –
For what? The craftsmen moles working away beneath
The earth to make a secret, sacred image
Of the world above; for what?
Did they believe that just as long
As this, their secret, magic simulacra survived,
All would be well? The great city above,
As long as their duplicate world still stood,
In sympathy, would still have life?

Perhaps they saw their folly at the end,
When the white invaders came
To raid and murder, conquer and destroy.
Did they then, their faith confounded,
Seal the cavern, kill the shamans,
Curse their costly, holy-city toy?

Perhaps. Yet we are at it too in our own way:
Seeking to deny, defeat the grave,
Searching for salvation in our own dark cave.
For centuries wise men in cloud-tall towers
With telescopes have burned away the days,
Scrying our grotto roof seeking the truth. And even now
With satellites and radio waves, they probe the skies;
Still looking for the lost key to the door,
The fine minds of our own world grub out their lives.

But in spite of all we are just where we were before.
Lying confounded on the cavern's bare, cold floor,
We stare at specks of Fool's Gold flashing in the night,
Convinced there is an answer to this mystery;
And all the while the unfathomable stars perplex the wise,
And hang like gewgaws in a children's nursery.

The Curve of Love

Stopped at the lights I watch the people cross –
A small town, summer morning, cloudless, hot.
Shopping trolleys, noses in iPhones, fast fingers text;
Overalls, short skirts, handbags, nice legs and next
A blind man with a stick. Then, last of all,
A dark-haired father comes bearing a small,
Blond child, a cloud of curls laid on his shoulder
Copper smouldering in the sun, red-gold.
Her arms slack down, her tiny bum
Safe saddled on his strong left arm,
And, light against her sleeping back,
His right hand keeping her from harm.

Were I a sculptor I could have caught it all:
That universal curve of love,
The little tummy snuggled in,
The fire-brass coils on his dark shirt;
That moment all of love was there,
Love shielding her from hurt.

Were I a painter I could then, with just
One stroke of my full-loaded brush,
Freehand, unrushed, perhaps
Have captured that most lovely line of arm
And child, that sleeping, trusting, wobbly head.

No chisel or paints, or skill with them,
I will make do instead with words.
For in that subtle, tender arc,
That shoulder and those curls –
The slow waltz of the stars,
The breath of all the worlds.

A Nocturnal Upon St Lucy's Eve

Manchester 2016

I

On Old St Lucy's Eve I sit, the sky a bruise,
The world on edge. I watch the news
In a downtown bar where cotton brokers
Once would meet to drink but now there comes
A different gang: new boys in town, the suited jokers,
Beyond all reach: the wilful deaf but never dumb.
Tonight they bray, slap backs, play-punch and jeer,
Depth-charging shots into their bitter northern beer.
Minted, flushed and flash they are dancing to
The algorithms of a different empire's drum;
Oblivious to the turning of the year.

The city gathers darkness like a shroud unto itself.
It pours it out in rivers, down cold streets,
Washes it down hidden lanes and alleyways.
It fills the walkways, colonnades, the quiet squares,
And pools it, snuffing out the candle of the day.
It is the kind of dark that sucks the light from everywhere –
From the terraces and library steps, the old chop house,
From the towpath and smokers' yard behind the bar –
And takes the city, slick and neat, a cat eating a mouse.

The suits scrum with a laugh into the night,
Ready for what comes: fly, fuck or fight.
The barman aims the remote, winds up the sound
And I see the world is bent once more on sliding down
The short, sharp road of malice and of hate;

In clouds of ignorance and winter dark
The lunatics have stormed the park
And are running now pell-mell in packs to shut the gates.

II

Something we thought had gone is come again
And is reborn with marches, street fights, arm salutes
And rabid posturing. The worst strut braggardly
Across the screen; the best, their voices smothered
By the screams of hate, sing canticles that go unheard.
A cartoon toff in a morning suit and an acid mouth
Sweats privilege from every pore; before the Golden Door
The velvet-collared thug and the lead thief meet
The Orange Clown in his Great Tower, on a lads' day out.
These are the new boys, come sudden on the block,
The puppet masters here again, come back to call the shots.
A sleeping beast? But did it ever sleep? Perhaps not.
Far easier to hate than love; to see danger, to keep
Alive fear of the helpless, hapless stranger. Heap
Them high – false myth, skewed fable, a false and curious
Narrative. 'Take back control. A glorious past.
Spitfires. Our borders, money, laws. Stabbed in the back.'
The honeyed, weasel words said often enough, chanted
Out loud enough will pick and drill and worm – like cankers.

A dose of fear, a peck of hate,
A drizzle of despair, a crust
Of lies and half-truths, just
What you need; that and
A smear of terror and a quart or two of cant.
And then the smoke and mirrors bogeymen
Can shark from out the dark,
And lead the lost just any way they want.

III

I watch the city slither towards the edge –
Like something blind or unaware:
The tribal laughter in the bar, smug boasts and howls
Of victory, the banter – there is something feral in the air.
We gambled but the dice were loaded;
The past a pageant now, the future not decoded.

And so we stand, astray, alone, apart,
Each day more filled with fear. The chart
And land no longer tally. We are here,
At the withered turning of the year,
No gods to which we can all kneel and pray.
The path behind is brambled now, each day
More rockfalls choke the valley way
Back home, and we seem lost.

We hear the chanting of the mob
As we stumble in the haunted wood;
The fear-dimmed sky darkens above –
All's left to light us home is Hope and Love.

Driftwood Maps

Sitting, fog-fast stilled, silent in his skin kayak,
Mute ice mountains slowly wallowing past,
The hoar-frost thick enough to chew, he clasps
The solid map. His hands slip out of his mitts
And stroke the piece of carved flotsam; fingertips,
Nipped by the icy air, decode the wooden chart.
They trace the inlets, calving glaciers, lacework reefs,
The sheer ice face, the harpoon rocks beneath
That would slice his flimsy craft apart.

This driftwood map, made by those gone before,
Reworked through ages as the coastline changed,
Shows him the scarp and scoop of every shore,
The cant of every cliff. Were he stone blind
He still could, like a homing salmon, find
Safe passage through the pack ice and the bears, alone,
To make landfall, to braille his way along the seal road home.

We have no such solid maps to navigate our seas, our bays,
Our world, our days; the sureties of dogma, creed and faith –
Blind alleyways – lead us astray. Our pilots now
(Sad captains with long-faded charts and sun-dimmed eyes)
Take us to the borders and the coasts of transient lands,
Decreed as absolute and by dictat defined,
With not one single thought of what lies out
Beyond the shifting contours of our two-dimensional lives.

We plough on in our passage from dark to dark;
Our little skin canoes, our brittle barques,
Roll and tremble as they are tumbled helter skelter

By the indifferent, brutal winds. There is no shelter
Now. Our shifting, shaking world, intangible
As mist, feels every whisper on the wind, is fragile
As blown blooms; it is a faded rose at dawn
About to slough and scatter on a summer lawn.

A Murano Dagger

*Give me the child for the first seven years and I will give you
the man.*

IGNATIUS OF LOYOLA

*The setting: Manchester. A religious retreat for schoolboys
at a convent. A golden afternoon in early autumn, 1959.*

1 The Introibo

Starched wimples sail above low bushes like
Barge canvas, luffed and crossing the low fens.
Sedge rustles, first Fall leaves lie and rot
Where water laps at the pool's still edge.

A whisper of wind shimmies the surface, daps
A cloud of flies, Dark Olives, a late hatch.
Along the narrow path, where the sisters go,
Sea-green bushes tremble to far traffic,
A distant rumble in this place; the world
Beyond heard only as a troubled undertow.

Brass bombs of carp burnish the deeps,
Rising to a novice hand, which casts a neat
Arc of stale bread upon the waters.
Praying, silent, Rome's daughters
Thread the quiet, Victorian gardens;
The high wall of the Italianate convent marks
The limits of their lives. The melody beyond,
In that uncharted, troubled sea, is here tacet,
A cove out of the clamour and swell,
Hushed haven from the harrying world.

Brides of the carpenter, they keep their tryst,
Bound willing by their vows,
They usher quietness in this gathering ground.
Here whispering voices, murmur words
Tinged with the *blas* of hay-times in a Sligo field,
A schoolroom in West County Clare,
Net mending on a wind-buffed Donegal strand.

The prefects line the blazered ranks
Outside the door. Boys shove, cuff, yank,
Nudge, pinch, squeeze, roar, dig, curse, poke,
Twist, push, knee, stamp – until a shadow crow
Stooping along the path shivers them to stasis.

As the priest glides past, his cassock swirls
A train of leaves; crisp turnings
In his wake are scattered, the first
Blood-bright rust of the year. Pew bound,
Prayer books in hand, the daily round
Begins; the boys shuffle dully in
Heads bent in bogus piety. They kneel
In silence yawning, school-caps under knees,
As the servers enter and the priest,
Vested in gold thread and silk, intones.

Introibo ad altar Dei
I will come unto the altar of God.

Servers, too young for irony, respond
In flat Mancunian drones,

Ad Deum qui laetificat juventutem meam
To the God who brings joy to my youth.

II The Credo

Confíteor Deo omnipoténti:
Mea culpa, mea culpa,
Mea máxima culpa.
I confess to Almighty God
Through my fault, through my fault
Through my grievous fault

Clouds rive, sun falls in glory
Through the high stained-glass,
Washes the chapel floor
With a pool of rainbow light.

He kneels, fair hair, blue eyes,
The ghost of a moustache on his top lip;
His voice splintered, a lost boy, islanded by guilt.
The river of Grace flows past unhindered,
His sins snicker, snake-slither, slide
Smooth as a Murano dagger between his ribs;
Once in, the twist is made, the thin, glass blade
Snapped off remains to work its way
In deep, to sour and wound a little more each day.

Glória in excélsis Deo. Et in terra pax
homínibus bonæ voluntátis.
Laudámus te. Benedícimus te. Adorámus te.
Glory to God on high. And on Earth
Peace to men of goodwill.
We praise thee. We bless thee. We adore thee.

The organ flutes, nuns' high voices ring
Amongst the alabaster saints,
The painted plaster virgins; descant,
Boys' crackling voices chant

As Christ looks down, stands,
Heart-in-hand above
The burning sacristy lamp.

Credo in unum Deum. Patrem omnipoténtem,
Factórem cæli et terræ.
I believe in one God. Father almighty.
Creator of heaven and earth,

Only, the boy has doubts; still half a child,
Burdened with sin, awakening to the world,
Trying to fathom its complexity and pain.
Hiroshima, Belsen, Auschwitz, Nagasaki;
The ovens, those mass murdering bombs – again
And again he asks the priests, where then was God?
They tell him it's a Mystery; God gives us choice.
And do we choose, he asks – plague, cancer,
Famine? Choose to be born blind or deformed?
Why does the hand of God,
The voice of God not call an end to all
The suffering? They smile, tell him he's young,
And sing the song they long have sung:
God's way, His wisdom, He knows best
Praise Him; Pray to the Holy Ghost.
That He will send the gift of Faith
He prays to the emptiness
And the emptiness echoes.

Sanctus, sanctus, sanctus,
Dóminus Deus Sábaoth.
Holy holy holy,
Lord God of Hosts.

The altar cloth, starched, immaculate, holds
The wine and water, and the inky fingers of
The altar boys are curled round gold

And precious stones. Offertory bells
Tell that the mystery is done,
And Christ has come to Earth again.
Flakes of light, sparked from the gold and gilt,
Dapple the chapel walls, flames of the Paraclete.

III   Communion

Hoc est enim corpus meum.
For this is my body.

Arabian frankincense perfumes
The air, nuns bow their heads,
Beat breasts; lips move, sigh,
As the host and chalice are raised high

Quod ore súmpsimus, Dómine,
puramente capiámus,
et de múnere temporáli fiat
nobis remédium sempitérnum.

What has passed our lips as food, O Lord,
May we possess in purity of heart,
That what has been given to us
In time may be our healing for eternity.

Tongues take unleavened bread, host to the host,
The living God lodged in the mouth's soft sepulchre.
Hot beeswax drips, flames bob and dip,
Jig in the half-light and are mirrored to
Infinity in chalice, plate and candlestick.

He kneels and takes the bread,
Body of Christ, into his mouth,
Knowing it is a foul ash-pit.

His soul is in a state of Mortal Sin;
He made a bad confession, hid
From the priest: the girl, the things they did.
He takes upon his tongue no paper thin white host;
Instead the one-way ticket to the Hell he chose.
A sin against the Holy Ghost, the certainty
That he is damned. No help, no healing for eternity;
He feels the Hound of Heaven's burning breath,
And sees God's hollowed palm – a bunched, tight fist.
Outside, beyond the walls, the smoke, the prayers,
The burning brass and gold, bells ringing,
In all the trees the chapel birds were singing
And calling down damnation in the free, blue air.

Ite Missa est.
Go, the Mass is ended.

The nuns file out, hands clasped,
Eyes on Pugin's encaustic tiles,
Their heavy bone beads rattle
As a prefect rings the chapel bell.
The boys stay, captive, strangely quiet,
Wait for the mission priest to turn the day to night.

IV The Jesuit

He marches in, a small whirlwind, brisk, soldier-like
And Irish. Young, with steel-rimmed glasses; eyes
Hard, sea-green; ginger, close-cropped hair.
His knuckles grip the pulpit, and his voice stabs at the air.

'We meditate, today, boys, upon Christ's Calvary,
His death, His sacrifice, His life offered to purge
The sin of our first parents, Adam and Eve,

The Sin of Knowledge that damned all the Earth.
His redeemed gift to us, a choice: of life eternal
Or the everlasting torments of the depths of Hell.'

He takes them swiftly from the trial – Pilate,
Barabbas – to the scourging and the mountain's foot.

'Imagine, boys, the pain, the thirst, the skin flayed by
The whips, salt in the wounds, the heavy, rough-hewn cross
Tearing our loving Saviour's skin through to the bone.
See how he stumbles, falls to rise again
And stagger through that searing terrible heat,
Climbing that torturous hill of death. Think on
The dust, his bare feet slashed by razor rocks,
That cruel crown of thorns, the blows,
The knocks and kicks, the mocking mob's wild hate,
The jeering spittle dribbling down his lovely face.
Imagine the fearful, unendurable pain
As soldiers hammer in the nails. They tear straight
Through our Saviour's palms and feet.'

He pauses, to let the story sink deep down,
Planting his words like blows upon the blameless air.

'Do you not care? Do you not know,'
He raised the storm, 'How every sin
That you commit is yet another blow; sends fresh
Infinities of nails into your Saviour's flesh?
It is not Jews alone that crucify your Lord,
But you, who each and every day renew his Calvary.
Is not one death enough for you, but that you drag
Our Saviour up that cruel mount and crucify
Him each and every hour of every day?

But the time will come when the horn will sound
Three blasts from that great horn and all will end –
Time is, time was but time shall be no more.

Every soul that was and is will stand
Before the Lord with Jesus at his right hand.
When judgement comes, what will you have to say
As you stand there before him? How will
You account, what will the scales tell?
No hiding then, all will be out
Your sins will shout to the skies.'

Silence. A boy coughs. A trapped wasp fizzes
Against a window glass. The moment passes.

'With every filthy thought you harbour,
Rolling in it like a pig in its own filth;
With every lustful look, each impure deed,
You drive in the spear, and hammer in the nails.
Look at Him now, boys, strung up on the cross.'

His arm sweeps wide, points to the crucifix
Christ hanging, head down, near the end;
Painted Italian plaster, a dying man with a beard,
Nails, a spear wound; on his cheeks, glass tears.

'See how He weeps for you. When will your greed,
Your pride, your lust, your self-love cease
From nailing him onto that cruel tree?
When will you end this never-ending butchery?

Think of his last hours, the dust, the heat,
The vinegar on the scornful sponge;
The hard-caked blood, that wicked crown
Of thorns. Think how each time
You sin you ram those cruel spikes down
Deeper into our Blessed Saviour's skull.
Think of the lovely eyes, that looked
On all Mankind with love, blinded by gore.
Think of the sun hammering down
Out of that Golgotha sky, think of the time

MIKE HARDING

57

He hangs there, the Son of God, waiting to die.
The day crawls on, his sweet face black with flies,
While underneath, the soldiers gamble for
That one-piece cloak his mother-made.'

The wasp, demented, rages against the pane,
Falls and flies battering, helpless again.

The boy saw all his sins spread out before him,
A newsreel screening in a loop, round and round;
Ending always with his rotting soul Hell-bound.
The stinking sins he'd hidden from the priest,
The shame that mocked him, dragged him down.
He saw it all enacted time and again:
The kissing hungry mouths sucking,
Tonguing, longing in the after-cinema dark;
His pilgrim hand had roamed freely and found
Soft cotton, nugget nipples, cool skin,
Breast and mouth, drenched fingers,
Her hand guiding his to her tight-curled mat,
Her soft hot slit. Back-alley love,
Under a paper moon.
Knees jigging in the eager dance he could not stop
Of fumbled hot undoings and the sudden gouts
That splashed onto her stocking tops.
And he saw each thrust a thorn-spike hammering home,
The mocking thorns; each guilty groping fumble
Filled the sponge with vinegar, as he,
With only Heaven watching,
And three dustbin-throned cats,
Crowned Him and crowned Him
And crowned Him yet again,
Away from the dull streetlight;
Another Peter, thrice denying
Well before the cock crowed
On that moonlit summer night.

He stared, head bent, at the wood before him,
Pitch pine pew, the rail the colour of old blood,
Lit by a stained-glass fire, it was
The only answer to his questioning eyes.
He felt the guilt rise, lapping deep within;
A lake of vomit, sour and curdling,
Reaching for his gorge. Christ on the cross
Because of him. Christ's mother's agony
Because of him. The soul that will be lost
Through his fault that lost it on that moonlit night.

'Boys, you are growing, soon you will be men
The sin of lust will tempt you more each year;
You needn't fear, boys, so long as you pray
To the Blessed Virgin every day.
She will help you when you need her most,
But turn against her and you will be lost.
Christ's mother is of a purity unblemished.
The sinless one, conceived without the stain
Of original sin on her immortal soul.
Virgin most pure, she watches over you all,
Sees everything you do, and, when you fall,
Her sad heart fills with sorrow. Pray to her,
Boys, for the sake of your immortal souls.'

v   The Nunc Dimittis

'Go now and spend the hour that's left in thought
And meditation, thinking on Christ's sacrifice.
Now we will say the prayer to the Mother of God
You first learned at your own dear mother's knees.'

Hail Mary, full of grace, the Lord is with thee.
Blessed art thou among women, and blessed is the fruit
Of thy womb, Jesus. Holy Mary, Mother of God
Pray for us now, and at the hour of our death. Amen.

MIKE HARDING

He leaves just as he came,
Missal under his arm,
Blows through the door
A soldier in God's war;
Letting the Heaven-Hound
Roar through the opened door.
It searches the chapel round,
Its breath the stench
Of snuffed church candles,
Stale frankincense.

The boy sees it and it trails him
From the chapel through
The home-time afternoon
And mindless chatter.
The boy is dumb, blighted by a darkness
That the journey home across the town
Is powerless to scatter.

And after – sick-full, long nights
Of terror and dark dreams.
He knows there is no hope for him.
In a state of sin, he took Christ's body,
Knowingly. Like Luther, there is no return
He is on a railway track, one way
And no way back, no help,
Night coming and no lights burn
Up ahead, just steel rails shining in
The dim starlight; and at the end,
Hell, Satan and all the Devils.
He has seen enough of Bosch to know
What lies in store, for evermore.
And his mother will see, his family
Will see, his friends all see,
His teachers see – his caustic sins
Will reel before them, flickering frames
Will lay bare, all he has done. Shamed.

He then begins the long years cloaked
In the lie, the second skin that hides
Who, what he is. Not here, not him,
Not part of their life, not he: the mask is on.

And Satan's dance of triumph kicks out sparks,
That sear his soul. He feels the fell of dark
Down all his restless nights, and wakes
In rigid terror knowing that, no matter
What he does, Hell is where he is bound.
The black Hound follows him
Down all the days, casts him away
From family, from friends. And even though
With time he finds at last his own way out
Of the labyrinth of Rome and can disprove
The dogma and the Humpty Dumpty words,
The structures, power and pomp;
And believes that he has killed the Minotaur –
Like Pavlov's dog, the sound of Sunday bells,
The smell of frankincense, the Latin Mass,
Conjures the wasp battering the glass
And gibbering demons calling out his sins;
He feels always the keen Murano blade,
Still doing its work, lodged deep within.

*Note – The island of Murano, in the Venetian lagoon, is
famous for its skilled glassmakers. As well as beautiful go-
blets, bowls and plates they made thin glass stilettos, specially
designed to slide between the ribs of a victim. Once there, a
simple twist would leave the blade stuck deep in the victim's
body, with almost always fatal results. They were the preferred
weapons of many assassins.*

Sweetheart

'Sweetheart',
She called him.
In her eighties
Still a busy hen,
Pushing him on through
The morning town.
He, almost ninety,
Falling apart,
An old clock winding down,
Her 'Sweetheart'.
In a wheelchair,
Drooling and foggy,
Hardly there.
But yet what care, what love
Brimmed and bloomed
As she stopped and bent
And gently smoothed
And fluffed his thistledown hair.

Her tired voice, her crooked spine,
Her fallen flesh, her watery eyes;
She tidied the rug about his legs and
Smoothed it round with shaking hands.

And her soul said 'Yes, Yes, Yes!'
And again, 'Sweetheart,' she said,
Just that, and he smiled,
And nodded and she wheeled him on.

And that moment was not lost –
And oh, how beautiful it was.

Fír Na Mappa

For Tim Robinson – 'The Man Of The Map'

A net of names and lines snares sea, stories and land,
Transmutes them, sets them down upon the folding world.
The tales weave and web, the words
And shading hold the shifting landscape for a span,

Calling ghosts in from the dark heart of the bog.
They come, pale phantoms trailing stories
Made stronger by the telling: the land's log,
The lore, a whispering, closer than history.

Here's *Foxes Island* where Old Reynard
Licked a limpet, it locked down and held him hard
Trapped fast by his tongue until the tide closed in
And snuffed him out, his firecoal coat and all.

There the *Peelers' Steps*, the low-tide ford
Where the elusive *poitín* makers could be warned,
And all be off, quitting the still before the law
Came running, only to find smoking ashes, coil and mash.

Here is the *Half Way House* where murder lay
For peddlers and for pipers on the Old Bog Road;
A *síbín* where throats were cut and silver stowed from sight,
Deep graves cut in soft peat by lantern light.

He lined out every bay and inlet, curve and cove;
Half a life walking each inch along that ragged coast.
He leaves behind a hill of words and lines:
Connemara mapped out in the contours of the mind;

MIKE HARDING

The unwritten chronicles of a people laid,
In print; the palimpsest of the land with all its tales,
Its myths and legends, the secrets hoarded fast beneath
Like bog oak or bog bodies embalmed by the peat.

The buried legends were opened to the sunlight
By the *sleán* of words and line, telling their tales again
To the resurrectionist's ear, the bright
Eyed, mapper-storyteller's steel-nibbed pen.

Unity Mitford's Dream

Her parents, Lord and Lady Redesdale, liked to boast that
Hitler's favourite English rose had been conceived in the unlikely
sounding town of Swastika, Ontario.

In her silk pyjamas, supine on her bed,
Right arm, stiff, priapic, raised above her head,
Unity screeched, 'Heil Hitler' quite loud, every night;
Then, sighing, with a roll, turned off the bedside light.

To sleep? Perhaps to dream of her salvation
In Adolf's arms and of his coming glory,
The waves of roaring thousands and the story
Of the coming Reich the pure, new Aryan nation.

Jew-hater and Jew-baiter, did she jackboot in her sleep,
Goose stepping with the troopers, this Valkyrie?
Counting cocksure ss officers instead of sheep?
Dreaming of the Führer's mountain eyrie?

War declared, she lost the last crumbs of her mind,
And put a bullet in her head – Munich, September '39.
Strings pulled, lived on eight years, died in the country of her
    birth,
And lies now with her sisters in the rich, red Cotswold earth.

Mad, bad and sad, her bizarre story now
With all its 'It Girl' glamour shows us how
The great string-pullers play with loaded dice,
And have always, ever, skated firmly on thick ice.

And we below them gaze at the frozen ceiling, yearning
While the great cogs roll through all our days,
Meshed above our powerless heads always;
They gyre relentless, ever grinding, churning.

And Unity Mitford goose-steps through her dreaming,
Remembering the party where they forced 'the Sheenies'
Down on their hands and knees like sheep to eat the grass.
Oh how, they had laughed, and oh, how she had laughed.
And Unity turns over, smiling, chuckling in her sleep
As the gangs of glass-breakers come marching through
    the streets.

Hindu Kush Moon

Once in the Hindu Kush I watched
The full moon climb above a mountain pass,
Lighting the horned seracs –
The penitents that sentineled the glacier.
Then the river came quicksilver as
The limelight noosed our camp
And turned our tents to bleached
Cocoons pitched on the river's bank.

The beauty of that moon-glazed land
Lies in my mind's eye still,
As does the beauty of the people of the hills
Who nursed and lugged me down half-dead
From the high pass when I fell ill;
Dog-sick with dysentery, so sick,
Not caring if I died or lived.
Five days of curds and honey and sleep
Before I was back again on my unsteady feet.

Now in this northern English city's streets
The same old moon lifts up its innocent face
Between the horns of the Market's
Glass and concrete cocks. While
Somewhere, in some other place,
The rockets and the drones are being primed.
And soon those hill tribe's at home
Asleep, the children softly breathing,
The men who carried me, sleeping,
The women who fed me, sleeping
In their mountain villages made
Of mud, and stones and sticks.
All of them will soon be scattered meat
And ragged hanks of hair and bone,

Lives sundered by a politician's cant,
Some merchant banker's balance sheet,
The waving of a Texas oil man's
Manicured and gold-ringed hand.

And the man who piloted the drone,
In a cool room in Nevada, half a world away,
Will aim his paper coffee cup at the trash,
Lock down the console, pull his jacket on,
Remember it's his turn to get the kids,
And, noting how it is so unseasonably hot,
Will stroll out to his white Toyota SUV
Across the baking tarmac of the parking lot.

Mythologies

For the ones just here and those that are to come.

I

Your great-great-uncle Bernard once, in Bangalore
Just as the Japanese were taking Singapore,
Rode a piebald pony up the marble steps
Of the porticoed and stuccoed officers mess,
For nothing more than 'fun',
Half-pissed and running on anarchy and rum.
Got jankers, forty days, and lost his stripes
But didn't give, he said, 'a flying shite'.
A starving beggar woman cursed him
When he threw her not rupees
But worthless farthings – and he knew
No luck from then until his death.
Fell in a pit of cobras on a jungle march
(My nanna saw him in her dreams)
A flat-necked, serpent king, bejewelled
Rearing up above him. So she prayed
To the Blessed Virgin, just one mother
To another, to save him from an Indian grave.
Next day a squad of Gurkha angels
On a jungle march came on the pit
And Uncle Bernard's life was saved.

Your great-great-uncle Harry, ginger haired,
Stole food from market stalls as a young child
To keep the family fed. Witty and wild.
Manchester Irish, in the Long Range Desert Group
He drove behind the lines of Rommel's tanks, a troop
Of phantoms ghosting in the frosty desert night
To blow up roads, airfields and ammo dumps.

Was bitten twice by scorpions (showed me the scars)
Once carried Randolph Churchill, half-pissed, to his car.
He ran a mobile snack bar in the town after the war
Then turned his smile and wit to flogging things:
Carpets and three-piece suites on Cheetham Hill –
Many there remember 'Harry Carpet' still.
Boxed for the army, and at sixty-three
Was cautioned by a judge for beating up three men
Who had attacked him in the street.

Your Irish great-great-great grandmother, so they say,
Was transported back to Ireland from Botany Bay,
Back to the land of scholars and of saints
From the land of the eucalyptus and the kookaburra –
Nelly Quinlan killed a man who tried to rape her –
A feisty woman, not wanted in Australia,
She sailed back home and here we are.

Your great-grandfather Norman,
Card-carrying Scouser, 'Snowy', spent his war
A signaller in minesweepers,
His small boat cleared the way
For the Allies to take Italy. Sorrento Bay,
So scummed and scurfed with bodies on that day
So thick they made a human causeway path;
'You could have walked across them to the shore,' he said,
    that memory was with him to the last.

Your great-great-uncle Jimmy on your grandma's side,
Rear-gunner in a Lancs, sat fixed for frozen hours riding
The skies in his cramped perspex cage, watching Orion,
The Plough and the Great Bear spool overhead;
'God's Dust' he called that scattering of countless suns.
But he looked always for the shadow, the brief
Mote or beam in the eye's corner, of death
Falling from above or sliding gently underneath.
Tail End Charlie, smart as paint he broke the bank;

With his brylcreemed parting and his 'tash;
Against the odds, he took the chance
And lived to tell the tale. And how he loved to dance
And sing, with Joannie waltzing round the kitchen,
Chairs pushed back, a crate of India pale ale
Brought home from the pub; and sing!
Lord how they made that little house ring!
Crooning Yankee songs laced with a dash of Scouse.
'Give us an old one, Jimmy!' 'Barefoot Days',
'Heart of My Heart', 'Who's Sorry Now?'
And last of all, always, the Maori anthem of their war,
'Now Is the Hour', lifted to the rafters.
I'd stand outside on stardust nights
And see that council house its windows all on fire,
Gifted, chock-full of love and laughter.

Great-great-uncle Jack crewed on convoys,
Merchant ships from Liverpool, Scouse boys,
Out on the seal-grey, slaughtering Atlantic Sea;
The wolf-pack subs picked them off, easy
As drowning kittens in a tub.
But somehow, Uncle Jack was off the killers' sights,
Torpedoes passed him by, night after night,
And he too came back home to sing and laugh
With Aunty Eileen and to work with Jimmy
On the Black Stuff, on the 'Trinnie',
Their war as unreal now as a journey to the moon;
His religion, Liverpool, his family
And Anfield every Saturday afternoon.

Your great-grandma Kay plotted out the course
Of bombers, counted out then counted in
The Brylcreem Boys. One could well have been
My dad, a Devon boy from Ottery, Louis –
A navigator in Lancasters who, night after night,
Flew over Germany, Angel of Death,
With flak coming up so thick and dense

You could have danced the tango on its burning floor.
Nine Squadron flying from Bardney, Lincolnshire
They flew to Archangel to bomb the Tirpitz in its fjord.
He fell one September night, on fire, like Icarus,
Wings melted not by the sun but by a German ace
Nachtjäger pilot, Heinz Schnaufer; and so he went
Down with his crew to Holland's polders, fens and dykes.
In Holten village churchyard now he lies.

Great-grandma Eileen was my mum,
Heavy with me when my dad fell from the sky.
Five foot and a tea leaf, a Land Army girl
Somehow handling shire horses,
Sang her days away. Read poetry
To me and taught me songs, never afraid of work.
Somehow we managed. Christmases
We made our decorations from crepe paper,
Flour paste and tinsel. New Year's Eve I went out
The back door, knocking on the front with coal
And salt and bread, for luck and plenty in the year
To come. A lifelong Socialist,
Stood at Greenham with her women,
Arm-in-arm, a human chain, circling the pods of hate.
She married a Pole, Big Lou, one of Anders' men;
Tank driver in the war, he fought for us
Across Europe then worked his life away
To keep us all. Spoke broken English all his life.
His family, his allotment and ten bob a week
To play the horses was his world, that and
His Polish newspaper and friend, another Pole, Bruno,
Who played the accordion and had cut the throats
Of Panzer troops on the slopes of Monte Cassino.

This is your blood, these are those gone before,
Whose names, whose tales you carry;
The ones, once young, who walked the long path
You are walking now, who stepped

Aside to let you journey on.
These are your legends, your mythologies
As real as any baronet's blood lines
Or hallowed family trees. We have
No marble tombs, no alabaster knights,
Their dogs curled at their feet, their gauntlets
On their swords, their wife's
Hands clasped in prayer, staring dauntless at
The silent, musty, chapel's cobwebbed roof
With blank unseeing eyes. Instead we have
This cairn of words, this roll call, these annals
Of the ordinary, most extraordinary
People in the world; who flew like birds,
Who crossed the seas, who loved and laughed,
Who sang and talked; whose stock
Was Irish, English, Romany and Scots;
Who walked the long ways down the lanes of mystery.
These are your bones, your blood, your gone-befores,
Your lineage, your people and their history,
And these – the stories and the songs they'd sing –
As rich and wonderful as any lord's or King's.

The Long Acre

'They are grazing the long acre,' said of travellers' horses on the verge of a road.

Their horses still stand patient on the grass,
Just as they did a thousand years ago.
Tethered, grazing; cars and trucks roll past;
On the summer air the blue bloom of woodsmoke.

An old man sits on his van steps taking the sun,
Clothes dry on the hedge, the travellers come together
Round the fire. The world goes turning at a run,
And year on year the gypsies come as ever

They have done. Down old backroads
And lanes, they trundle, raggle taggle,
With their cobs and bow-top wagons,
On their way to fairs, horse sales, to deal and haggle.

The have made their camps for centuries, their fires
Lit all the old long acres of the world.
A thousand years they have been travelling here,
They see things differently, their eyes

Still looking, fixed on far horizons
See the resting places, *atchin tans*,
They live within a shadow world that others cannot see,
Still read and speak the language of the land.

Look for the Long Acres as you pass along the way.
They're hard to find unless you have an eye
To see; twin oaks will mark the place a child has died,
Two acorns buried with it in the grave.

They have a world apart that few can understand,
A country lost to us, yet one that once we knew,
When our fore-elders tramped the empty lands;
For in the wakening dawn of time, weren't we
    travellers too?

Dancing at the Cosmic Ceilidh

'Mike, where did yesterday go?' – Tobias, age 4

The poster on the parish noticeboard,
Underneath the dog mess warning
And the Methodist Love Feast
Poster for the coming Sunday morning,
Was an invitation to a spree.
It stated baldly there would be:
'A Dance to The Slow Music of Time'
They lied, oh how they lied.

Slow? You must be joking, for
When 'Tempus and The Fugiters'
Take the old bandstand,
The more the years go by
The faster plays band.

They play every damn gig there is
As though they all are drunk
And we are paying the band
(Wink, wink, tap-nose) with cash in hand,
To speed the damn thing up.
So round and round we go,
Learning to love the spin we are in
Under the old dark magic of farce.

First the fiddler's elbow
Goes like a lover's arse,
Then what started as a waltz becomes a jig.
And the banjo player's fingers flutter
Like fat, pink, manic spiders,

And the skin upon his banjo starts to smoulder.
We all dance on, a little older
And a hornpipe morphs into a Kerry polka.

The box player's playing fit to rip his bellows,
And the bodhran player
(A big, Connemara fellow
Good player and a joker)
Has got the goatskin bleating,
And turns the reel into a tarantella.

And then, just as Mother Brown's
Knees have Hokey Cokeyed down,
And you are sweating,
Heading for a breather and 'a wetting'
In the cool, dark refuge of the bar,
The dance-hall doors spring wide ajar.
The spangling mirror ball sparkles die,
And out there, before you, it all lies
Stretching out into night, forever more:
Nothing but whatever with the stars for floor.

The melodion wheezes out a chord,
The fiddler fine tunes his A-string, bored;
And the eternal banjo player gives a call,
'Right, let's have you on the dance floor, all
Of you, both great and small, this is your final chance,
Between the jigs and the reels to kick your heels,
And join your partners for the last, last dance.'

The Price of Sugar

Oh lads, but weren't we splendid on the day the boats
Ran us ashore! The Jack Tars spat and cursed
And roared out, 'Lobsters!' at our crimson coats.
We drummed up the beach through the blood-warm surf
And bawled out 'Brighton Camp' in half-drunk chorus,
No laughing matter to the ones who saw us
Coming, marching up the strand, powder dry, steady,
And smart as paint – rum-brave and battle ready.

My first shots killed a Dutchman and his wife.
I cut their maid's throat with my boning knife.
(Five years a butcher's boy – you don't forget.)
I staved a small boy's head in with my musket butt;
One blow, his skull cracked like a nut.
Four fine, mulatto doxies in a yard,
We fucked them while the corporal stood guard.
Then we killed them, torched the huts;
Moved on, necked a flagon of rum –
Hot work all that killing under that big sun –
The stink of burning hair and flesh would turn your guts.
A mob of coloured birds chuckled high above the smoke
As though we had just cracked the most enormous joke.

Our frigate loosed its canons on the fort and town
And made a shambles of the governor's fine house;
Any that ran out we cut them down,
Destroyed them like you would a lop or louse.
Some lads smeared blood across their chops
Like savages. Such bedlam, boys, we ran amok!
And looting? Hell, we got some stuff!
Fine silks, gold rings and Dutch tobacco, rum and snuff.

'Go for it lads,' our sergeant said. 'Just fill your boots.'
And that we did. Ran up the Union Jack, got royal drunk.
'This is one for history,' said Drummer Monks.
'They'll write this down in their great printed books.'
Dodds, on the drum head, divvied up our loot
While Sam played 'Polly Oliver' sweetly on his flute;
With more of the Dutchman's rum, we toasted our
    good luck –
That night we got too drunk even to fuck.

Next dawn I was hog-sick. I spewed my ring
Into the ashes of the huts, they were still smouldering.
Head banging in a ran tan, here against my will;
Just doing my job: like all of us, brought here to kill.

King's Shilling?
Aye, in the bottom of an alehouse pot.
But still, God willing,
I'll get home with the eyes 'n legs 'n arms I've got.

And here we sits and flaps our wingsalum,
Flaps our wingsalum, flaps our wingsalum,
And here we sits and flaps our wingsalum,
Down in Demerara.

Warm Summer Grass

Warm summer grass, a bed for loving on,
And all the time at all to do it in.
Long afternoons and evenings of love,
We crushed the grass in secret hollows
High up on the hill; nobody would
Find us way up there, no one would follow.

We thought we'd all the time in all the world
But, all the time, the world had all the time.
Still, as small clouds rolled and furled,
And reddened in the dying sun, weaving
The years ahead, that grass bowl would hold
Us until the stars pricked out bright holes
In the darkening summer sky.

The scent of those warm, sweet, crushed grass days
Had us then and has me still;
Never the scent of new mown hay
But that, wherever I am, it is that summer hill.

The Paths

These are our stories scribed into the earth:
The scrimshaw of a people's feet, the tracks,
The timelines made through all our days:
The path the children cut to walk to school,
The posties' way, the line the quarrymen cut
Crossing the moor, 'the monks trod' paved
Across a Dales flood plain; the miners' paths,
The packhorse road, the Salters Way,
The road the marching legions hacked
Over the moors; and, long before,
The lines worn by the bare, cracked soles
Of tribes on pilgrimage to call the sun
Back with their fires into the ring of stones.

All these scratches made upon the glass of time
Are ways of telling and of being;
These are the people's chronicles,
As real as any book of words.
Ask me the legend of *The Old Corpse Way*
And the slabs of stone they'd set the body on
To take a rest and drink and get their breath.
Ask me the stories of the smugglers' paths
Used to bring the rum, silk and tobacco from the bay;
The Butter Tubs where they would trail
Across the watershed from dale to dale,
On market days returning by the light of the full moon:
Or *Gladys' Leap,* a postie's path and now a tune.
Close off the paths and what will there be left
Of all our stories and just who we were and are?
Shut down the old ways and you mute the tales,
The voices of just who we are; this is our litany
Carved on the land, our songlines and our history.

The Corrandrum Vase

Circa 1900–1800 BC. *Galway Museum.*

I

When did it dawn on us that we must die?
That there is darkness and an end to all?
That we will one day take a journey, each of us
To where the bones of Lazarus still lie?
When were we given the gift to see
Beyond the 'now', the simply 'being'
To what we know must surely come.

Not understanding how or why we're here
Or why we must all go, Straw Boys, Mummers
On the great stage of time, we play
At life, lost children in an empty house.
To candlelight the gloom we turned myth makers,
Who conjured up our gods in our own form.

They lived amongst the clouds on mountains,
Walked on water, raised the dead;
Fought monsters, made Creation in a week,
Hid in a burning bush. We moulded
Monkey gods and elephant gods,
A snake, an apple and a lost garden.
We made a league table of angels:
Thrones, dominions, archangels and cherubim,
Choirs and powers and seraphim.
To explain evil we made a would-be-god,
Upstart archangel; in our book
Lucifer, dawn-bringer, Morning Star.
Like children playing in a winter park
We cobbled stories out of fear
And terror of the endless dark.

Dogs do not see the end of days,
Try no more for immortality than a gnat,
A worm, a horse, a whale, a wildebeest or cat.
We also must have journeyed, for a while at least,
Unknowing, seeing our people fall like beasts
Along the hunter-gatherer track,
Leaving our dead where they fell, not looking back –
Once they were here, now they are gone.
Safe in our tribal groups we journeyed on,
Hunting, gathering, rooting out our food,
Roaming in packs, following the sun;
The conundrum surely never troubling us.

II

But then we come to findings like Corrandrum;
Sites where we made our funerary rituals, urn burials,
From simple tombs like here, a cist
To elsewhere: passage graves, wedge tombs, great tumuli
Raised up above the land around to hold
A mighty chief who nonetheless was levelled
By the spear of time. We buried them in splendour
With rich grave goods for the dead when they awoke
From what we must have trusted was but a sleep.

We buried with the husks that once had walked:
Gold cups, faience, glass beads, axe heads, torcs
Swords and shields, gold brooches, coral crusted pins,
Chariots, horses; cloaks, combs and rings;
Things of such great worth and beauty, artists' work,
Makings of many hands and hours, laid down with the dead
In great bell barrows. Did they, our ancestors, believe
The sun god, warming the chill, winter earth,
Would call the dead to rise again like barley,

The green, new shoots uncoiled, unfurled;
And did the Earth become the womb in which
We laid our dead, believing they would be reborn
After their death-winter in the underworld?
To live again for evermore?

Perhaps. But that black curse: the knowledge of the dark,
The never more? The prayers and stories made to light
The end of life, that endless night?
When did it come: the poison in the apple's core?
Ignorance, the wise once said, is bliss;
What would we give to unknow all of this?

Twitterstorm #Luther@Wurms

I

Ink and quill, velum, a nail, a Wittenberg church door
Were not enough alone to stoke the roaring
Fires, to screw the racks, to crack the legs,
Return the great abbeys to quarries;
Basket the heads of queens, roast abbots, parboil priests.
It was Gutenberg's small birds, the lead-cast beaks,
The moving type that pecked out all the codes.
It was the printer's devils with their sticks,
Their type, their hellbox and their inks.
The dead were butchered by the alphabet, by words,
By the printing presses' bright and terrible sword.

And when the little lead birds pecked,
Then dark blood stained the innocent page.

And, capering on its tarantella, out across
The world it went: Pandora's vented river of hate.
And the river became a sea, the sea a tsunami
That gathered strength from all it killed;
Whole towns and cities fell beneath the waves,
Like oats and barley ground relentless in a mill.
The old world's sureties were trashed,
The saints and angels torn and smashed,
Pulled from high niches in the abbey walls;
The stained-glass virgins, shattered,
The Christ child and the white dove scattered.
The Christian Taliban scraped away the hues
Of history, limewashed the past and made
The world anew in shades of puritan grey.

And the pyres of martyrs belched and thundered;
A world on fire, the stink of roast flesh everywhere
Perfuming town and city, market place and square.

And when the little lead birds pecked,
Then dark blood stained the innocent page.

A Treatise on This, A Counterblast on That;
The presses spread, and bred pamphlets and tracts
Thicker than fleas. The smallpox of rage
Raced down highways, crossed the seas, a novel plague,
New galliard of death, there were not graves –
Enough to hold the bitter fruits of hate. All life distilled
In this alembic to a binary, 'Yes' or 'No'.
Black rainbows spread across the Old World
While a righteous anger boiled and belched,
And sent its night-clad acolytes and nuncios,
Dark pilgrims all, sour-sailing out into the New.

II

Now it isn't paper, lead and ink;
Not presses, hot-cast type or binderies,
Not pecks – but pixels, bytes and binaries
The megabytes, the gigabytes, the terabytes;
There are, beneath the Earth, cities of silicon
And steel and glass; their algorithms hum,
Their smart brains cooled by fans.
It is a modern Pandemonium.
Fresh devils crunch infinities of numbers
To the beating of a totally new drum;
Spew images and words across the world
That leap and spin, outcry,
More numerous each nanosecond
Than the stars in the night sky.

And when the little pixels peck,
The blood of innocents spills out across the screen.

And, every second, hate and venom drool
From the half-made minds of clever fools;
Locked in the matrix, crystals glow
Fingers stab at keys and on it goes
Out across the world.
The box unlocked
once more, the ignorant and blinded weave
The warp and weft made from the pox
Of threads spun craftily by
Their one-eyed masters in the hidden halls;
The magi in their mansions who raise up false flags,
Turn round the signposts and then spin the rage
Anywhere but at the roots of the people's misery and pain.

We learn from history that not much has changed;
The puppet-masters are come back to tug the strings again
And all is never as it seems. The twitterstorms roll on,
Hatched by enchanters in their secret Sargasso,
And as before, nobody knows, no one can call
Which way the road will go, and whether there'll
Be racks and fires and gallows at the end of all.

And when the Piper's little pixels peck,
The blood of innocents spills out across the screen.

Undine – A Love Story

We feared old Jinny Greenteeth, all us kids;
My Nanna's fireside words conjured a water witch
Who lived in ponds and pitch-dark pools,
Fools swam too near her charms and slid,
Beguiled, clutched in her slimy arms to fathom down
As the world above them faded and they drowned.

But when I watched the swimming girls
Sun-flecked come slithering from
The broken surface of mill ponds,
Otter easy, water sloughing off
Their slim, pale thighs, their bathing suits,
Their skin blushed by the sun, I felt my roots
Stir and was shamed and couldn't name
The awakening in me.
And later came the Dales
That bike-ride summer; showing off,
The dizzy, puppy-dance of boy-lust
On the banks, the dive into the foss
As the summer light was lost
In the amniotic shadows of the deep stone bowl,
And everything was changed for ever
On the hot banks of that northern, summer river.

The men in black soutanes had said
'Thou shalt not!' But for me the dictat dread
Was fading, the plainsong dimming,
How could life and love itself be sinning?
And the girls, their siren smiles,
Their voices, water songs, light
And softer than starlight, music more sweet
Than any Credo, drowned the Paraclete.

Halfway up Kinder Scout there is a pool;
They say a naiad bathes there at full moon,
Croons and combs her long, gold tresses.
She is the mountain's and the moon's daughter;
She gathers moonlight in her hands
And scatters silver flakes across the rippling water.

For sixty years and more I have heard
That siren song, the watery laughter,
Marooned mariner, a swimmer in the tarn,
Half lost, I have ever followed after.

The Slap Bird

The ham-face leers, the hand a bacon bat, goes, *Slap!*
'There, that'll learn you!' says the priest. And then another:
   Slap!
And the small child weeps as his brittle, glass world splinters,
And the gentle summer's day turns dark winter.

And the slap flies out the window like an old black crow,
Waits on the schoolyard wall then tags the small child home;
Stays with him all the way through college, even goes
With the soutane and white priest's collar gifted him by Rome.

And then he too, in the holy name of power,
Will let the sin-black bird out free to flap and glower
And batter its black wings about another child,
To bring the curtain down, turn day to night.

Slap! Slap! On it merrily goes, the Misery Bird,
Making its demented way across the world.

Love on the Scarborough Train

Summer early morning mist, the sun a greasy
Burnished button. They got on at Leeds:
A clamorous crowd of children scurrying for seats;
Behind them women doing what they do so easy

And so well: herding the cloud.
Some are tots in trainers, ribbons, denim, loud
Little voices, Peppa Pig bags, unicorns, hair
In bunches and love set humming in the morning air.

Some are older; one with his Thomas lunch box
A red-haired boy, eight or so with rainbow socks,
A Leeds shirt and his kid sister,
A three-year-old in overalls

And a Little Mermaid tee-shirt.
Sand, sun, buckets, spades, and chips
A flock of wired, electric kids
And a day made bright with love.

Love by the bucketful,
Comes singing down through the air,
Burning hotter than the sun,
Stronger than the dark North Sea.

And the old train grumbles on towards
The coast, this carriage full
Of unspoken, elemental things:
Women with rough work hands,

Bleached hair, cheap clothes,
But hearts chock-full,
Racing to the coast for their day out.
The kids look out the window, shout

At the land that hurries them to the sea.
'We'll be there soon,' the red-haired little boy says,
And happiness comes rushing over all of them
Bigger than a rolling Scarborough wave.

Paddy's Rambles Through the Park

For Dezi Donnelly, fiddler and Man U supporter.

And so the tinker fiddler starts for home, the night
Starlit, the stars pulsing grace notes in the peat-black sky.
Halfway across the hill, the furze dusted with frost,
He finds himself inside a fairy fort – spell-fast and lost.

Far off he hears Atlantic combers meet the Donegal coast,
And smells, threading the wind, turf smoke,
Soft-blown from the old house where he played the dance;
But now he has crossed into another place, entranced.

No matter how he tries to turn and run and go
He finds himself ever captive in the great stone O.
Tin fiddle across his back he stumbles about that *rath*.
Each round tails back where he began; there is no path.

Then, *poitín*-legged and mazed, he hears the slow
Call of an air. Like no tune he has ever heard before
It comes up lilting from beneath the scattered stones.
A strain that tugs and holds him with its skein, its drone
And swirl; the savage beauty of its lonesome touch.
He rounds and scours the fort again seeking a cleft,
A gap, a way back home out of this other world.
But widdershins, always the music spins and skirls
And leads him on, one bar, one phrase, one step ahead.
Then he remembers what the old ones used to say
About 'the Stray' – to get out there is one way.

MIKE HARDING

He takes his jacket off and puts it back
On inside out and back to front,
And in minutes finds the hidden gap;
The moon rises to light his path
And he is gone, sprung from the charm,
And safe now from all harm.
But the music doesn't die, it lives on still
Singing within his head, as it did on the hill.

He hurries down the silent bends to home;
Once in his cottage door he takes the bow,
And the tin fiddle out and sends the tune
Swirling like sweet smoke round the room.
And ever after, wherever the old tinker goes
He tells the story, plays the long, sweet, *ceol si* notes.
The air that came, the gift unbidden,
The liminal, the numinous, the hidden.

Years later in an old stone Yorkshire house I hear
A young musician send the self-same tune
Flying out into the midnight air.
The fiddler, eyes closed, has found the truth
Of all the world, he has been gifted, touched.

We sense the music comes from somewhere else,
Somewhere beyond; and when he finishes – his last note
    the call
Of a wild bird or a dying star – there is not one of us
Who has not travelled too; and we stand lost, agog,
Touched by the frosty starlight on a Donegal bog.

Things You Will Never Know – #42

For Toby and Felix and IM *Robert 'Bobby' McLoughlin who took me there.*

This motorway you think was here since time began
Was once a dene where larks sang, field mice ran
Through ferns and brambles; there were bumble bees,
Hawks, hedgehogs, badgers, hares and centipedes.

A small child, running wild, I wandered here,
Picked ripe blackberries and mushrooms;
One summer saw great ranks, platoons
Of soldier orchids studding a high bank.
Here was a lake where the old headmaster
Heron on the pool's soft edge,
Hunched and shifty, stalked the sedge
For schools of gudgeon, perch and sticklebacks;
It's now a red brick maze of avenues and cul-de-sacs
With barbecues and trimly barbered lawns.
The city has moved out and taken it
In one unseeing and unfeeling yawn.

All gone the fields where they grew wheat,
The barley and the winter hay.
And for the rest? This retail park, back in the day,
Was acres of fat meadows filled with sweet,
Soft grass and shiny, brindle-coated cows.
This lorry park – two dairy farms,
This bowling alley – a pig farm and a lake,
This McDonalds drive-thru was a copse
Of silver birch, where once a big dog fox

And I outstared each other face to face
Until he realised I meant him nowt but good
And padded off again into the sheltering wood.

And here just where the motorway now dips
The deepest, once was marshland: rushy, pooled,
A childhood wilderness of sally, birch and fallen logs,
Dimpled with newts and loud with frogs,
Where water boatmen scudded on shallow ponds.

Look here, where the bridge's concrete piers
Hit bedrock and the culverts drain and spew
The motorway's runoff. Here was the pool
Now gone. I would come on summer days and lie
Here belly down and stare entranced.
Never anything so beautiful; my eyes
Filled with the flickering, shimmering dance,
The darting, sapphire sparks of damselflies.

Bells at Midnight – New Year – 2015

For Trevor Griffiths

The bells at midnight ring over the town,
Bells at midnight and the old year dead,
The new year wailing its way here, its head
Still covered by the caul of last year's stars.

People are on their knees across the land today
And few of them are kneeling down to pray;
The airwaves full of gibberish and spite;
Bread and circuses and unadulterated shite.

How long since the Finchley Housewife turned the crank
And opened up the gates, the flood that crashed the banks?
Remember it? Banging the Empire's one-skinned drum
She parroted trade and the flag, the oldest song around,
Yet brought both tumbling down.
A small-town shopkeeper's mind, frit of the folk-devils:
The General Strike, the hungry mob, the Jarrow men.
So she, the bit between her teeth, would see to it
The unwashed didn't climb back off their knees again:
Greenham, Orgreave, the dumping of whole cities in the bin,
Managed decline, Moss Side and Toxteth up in flames.
'Oi for England' tattooed on the fist
Of every young stormtrooper in the van,
And the family silver sold cheap to the candy man.

There were so many things we didn't see.
We took it read after the war
There had to be a better way.

But we reckoned without the cabal of power
That would make sure
That our dog didn't have his day.

The demob and rebuilding – how
The hospitals and schools stuck in
Their craws like bitter pills!
Jack and his master – they weren't having it
They didn't like that, not one little bit.

And from the last 'all clear'
The picking fingers, like green ivy
Started straight away to peck to bits
That modest heroes' world;
The change was changed, they saw to it.
A people hardly off their knees were soon
Back trying on their chains for a new fit.
And the ivy grew in strength until it had
Torn down the walls of that good world,
Had turned the lights out
In the sold-off children's ward,
And wound the fingers of the clock way back
To far beyond the place we all once were.

I think back on my people now all dead
And of their time, that other world,
Far kinder now it seems; as though it took a war
To teach us what our hearts and minds are really for.

This Morning *War and Peace* Was Sick

This morning *War and Peace* was sick.
Quite suddenly and without prior warning,
There came a noise like watery thunder
Followed by a projectile chunder
Which laid a half a million words or more
Upon the thick Axminster on the study floor.
'Get it up,' I said. 'You'll feel much better
In yourself' as an avalanche of letters,
A tsunami of Russian patronyms
Skelter-heltered off the shelf.

As kids in cars go copycat when one has spewed
So other volumes gagged – then quickly followed suit.
Proust was the worst, quite rude, impossible;
Heaving his past up, self-absorbed, unstoppable.
Lord of The Rings then coughed and hawked a scuttle full
Of ents and elves followed by a rake of trolls and orcs.
Then came *Don Quixote* close behind him,
And donkeys, windmills, lances all went flying.

Soon damn near every volume had thrown up:
Treasure Island – blank up to Ben Gunn,
Eliot's *Waste Land*, Shakespeare's Sonnets,
Winnie the Pooh, *Great Expectations*; on it
Went until I stood waist deep in words
Staring down and reading –

April is the cruellest dressing gown, ungirdled,
Stately, plump Poldy said, Yes Yes Yes.
Pieces of eight! Hold on tight, Prufrock!
You shouldn't have cut the Black Spot

MIKE HARDING

From Tigger's tum tum! Old Ben Gunn
Wants Christian bread and cheese.
What larks us shall have Pip when
The winter evening settles down with smells
Of cabbages and Kings, shall I compare thee to
A jar of honey? Busy old fool, unruly Sun
See Fluff run! Run Fluff, run!

I rang the fire brigade, spoke to the fire chief,
He said, Don't bother me.
We've a major, major, major tea party
With the March Hare at Bleak House and,
No lark rises and I know that this sounds absurd
But librarians everywhere are shovelling up tons of words.
Words in their millions in a rushing stream
I'm in the Slough of Despair, nothing does any good
Sherlock's drowned and all our candles
Have lighted fools the way to the woods.
Gregor Samsa dreamed he went to Manderley
On the day my grandmother exploded.
You can call me Ishmael; I am a camera
Slicing at the head of a moor.
Man Friday has come to bury Caesar,
This is the best of times, this is the worst of times,
I wandered lonely as a cloud to the Palace
With Alice to see the queen. She said,
Ask not for whom the bell tolls 'cos
The clock has struck thirteen.

A Letter from Connemara

I stand here on the island's west-most shore,
A bitten coast where bitter wrongs were done
Untrammelled. Here, god-armoured Oliver
Put thousands to the sword and, justified
By his iron-sided faith, he gave the poor
Who had no voice a Christian choice:
To Hell or go west to a Connaught grave.

A greater scar still marks the land,
An Gorta Mór[1] when a million starved to death
While, belly-full, the English ships
Sailed out with food, leaving the poor
Here in the west to eat grass in the ditch.
Two million fled, a million died,
Hardly enough left alive
To bury their own dead.

In my people's time there came
The murders in the mountains and the glens;
Brother against brother, massacres, men
Tied to landmines, blood drenched the quiet land.
Cities put to the torch, the Auxies and the Tans;
And later: barricades, the petrol bombs,
The knocks upon the doors at night,
The camps, the innocent dead,
The north a graveyard full of broken dreams
A borderland where fear ran like the Lurgan streams.

The rocks remember and the winds sing every day
The ballads of the broken bodies buried in the bog;

---

[1] *An Gorta Mór – The Great Hunger. The Irish famine of the late 1840s.
At least 1 Million died and 2 million emigrated to America or to the
mills and mines of England.*

The songs live in the marrow, are graven in the bone,
And the tales and myths are scratched upon the stones.

But then there came peace of a kind, a slow return
Down old lanes. The turf fires burn
In the hearths, there is a neighbourly coming home,
A kindly nod, the helping hand
A kind of healing on the land.

And now across the water we watch wires smoking
With rant and cant and insular drumbeats.
We see the men in suits, gaming the board,
Hear talk of them putting troops upon the streets.
Hate is spewed again against skin and poverty,
The crusted scabs of Empire brushed
Under the rug, questioners hushed
Called 'traitors'. In the border towns
And villages they wait and wait.
Smoke is puffed into the punters' eyes
And they spin the mirrors in the Great Mad Hall.

And here in Connemara we stand appalled
To watch a country turn itself
As those about to die do, to the wall.
It is easier to rule the people
Than to show them that they're ruled;
Always easier to fool them
Than to show them they were fooled.

Moon Over the Bens

Whatever science says, the moon tonight
Does have a human, smiling face
As it slides above the silver horns
Of the Connemara Bens. A Hunter's Moon, the light
Still dying in the west, casting a faint blush on
The hills; and time loops and I see
Before me that same Hunter's Moon,
In Hay on Wye, so bright it lit the road
Ahead as I drove to a gig some forty years ago.

That same old butter-faced moon
Once led me down through olive groves
In Cephalonia to a singing harbour bar.
That same moon shone on Tengboche,
Nepal, Mani Rimdu at the monastery,
Where a line of Sherpas sang and danced at the foot
Of ice-cowled Ama Dablam; that same old moon
Limelit Snow Lake in Baltistan, the ice
Endless it seemed, enough to swallow the whole world.

That same old friendly moon
Once took me down the bend for home,
Walking with me on a Ribblesdale road
From an old friend's house, my shadow
(Far more drunk than me) lurching ahead,
Waltzing wobbly down the shining way,
Lolloping through the mystery of this day-
In-night; the bright moon sailing
Over the Himalayas, Greece and Pen-y-ghent
Just as now it silvers the Connemara sky,
Touching the bright skirts of the hurrying clouds
With fingers of bright ice fire.

MIKE HARDING

Luath Press Limited

committed to publishing well written books worth reading

LUATH PRESS takes its name from Robert Burns, whose little collie
Luath (*Gael.*, swift or nimble) tripped up Jean Armour at a wedding
and gave him the chance to speak to the woman who was to be his wife
and the abiding love of his life. Burns called one of the 'Twa Dogs'
Luath after Cuchullin's hunting dog in Ossian's *Fingal*.
Luath Press was established in 1981 in the heart of
Burns country, and is now based a few steps up
the road from Burns' first lodgings on
Edinburgh's Royal Mile. Luath offers you
distinctive writing with a hint of
unexpected pleasures.
Most bookshops in the UK, the US, Canada,
Australia, New Zealand and parts of Europe,
either carry our books in stock or can order them
for you. To order direct from us, please send a £sterling
cheque, postal order, international money order or your
credit card details (number, address of cardholder and
expiry date) to us at the address below. Please add post
and packing as follows: UK – £1.00 per delivery address;
overseas surface mail – £2.50 per delivery address; overseas airmail –
£3.50 for the first book to each delivery address, plus £1.00 for each
additional book by airmail to the same address. If your order is a gift,
we will happily enclose your card or message at no extra charge.

Luath Press Limited
543/2 Castlehill
The Royal Mile
Edinburgh EH1 2ND
Scotland
Telephone: +44 (0)131 225 4326 (24 hours)
email: sales@luath. co.uk
Website: www. luath.co.uk